MY MOTHER'S BIBLE

 # 2

The Single Sermon Series

MY MOTHER'S BIBLE

by Pastor Sam Polson

Climbing
Angel
Publishing

My Mother's Bible
Written by Pastor Sam Polson

Transcribed and edited by Lisa Soland
Text copyright © 2023 Sam Polson

Published in 2023 by:
Climbing Angel Publishing
PO Box 32381
Knoxville, Tennessee 37930
http://www.ClimbingAngel.com

First Edition: May 2023
Printed in the United States of America

Cover photo: Shutterstock
Author photo: Stefan Holt
Graphic Design: Climbing Angel Publishing

ISBN: 978-1-956218-26-8
Library of Congress Control Number: 2023905603

This book is dedicated to godly mothers everywhere whose impact on so many lives is immeasurable. May God bless your incredible ministry.

I also dedicate this book to my wife, Susan, who has been a terrific mom, and three other specific mothers: one in Tennessee who chose life for her baby girl, allowing us to adopt our precious daughter, Ruth. Also, to a mother in Romania who chose life for her baby boy so that we could adopt our son, Stephen. And finally, to a mother in Indiana, who chose life for her child, and in time, that little girl could become our daughter, Jessica.

I am eternally grateful for these three ladies who chose life.

My Mother's Bible

I am ever grateful for my mother, who has been in heaven for nearly 18 years. She was a godly, committed Christian and a fine example for me, an impressionable young boy growing up with two older brothers in the small town of New Castle, Indiana. I loved my mother dearly and appreciate the opportunity to tell you a little about her.

My mom was a woman of many books. Due to her family's poverty, she could not attend high school but was a voracious reader with excellent knowledge. My brother and I used to say, "Boy, if we could just get her on Jeopardy, we'd get rich!"

But out of all the books my mother enjoyed, she was especially a woman of *the* Book. When I was a small child, I remember her setting a goal to read the entire Bible in one year. And she did that every year and sometimes twice a year for the rest of her life. I'm sure my mother read through the whole Bible over 50 times.

My mom wore out a lot of switches, and she wore out a lot of Bibles. I can assure you she believed in them both! The morning after my mother's passing, I noticed her Bible on the table beside her favorite chair. Looking through your mother or father's Bible after they are gone is truly an amazing and instructive thing. Inside the cover of my mom's well-worn Bible, she had written these words that I am using as the outline for this book. In her own shaky handwriting of her later life, my mom wrote these three short statements:

It's the blood that makes you safe.
It's the book that makes you sure.
It's obedience that makes you happy.

Amen, Mom!

We are told in Exodus 12:13 that the Lord spoke to Moses, giving instructions for the people of Israel (who were slaves in Egypt) to prepare them for that first Passover. Moses shared the Lord's promise, "The blood shall be a sign for you, on the houses where you are. And when I see the blood, I will pass over you, and no plague will befall you to destroy you when I strike the land of Egypt."

This promise was given during the time of God's judgment on Egypt. With a hardened heart, Pharaoh continually refused to let God's people go. After nine dreadful plagues, God declared He would bring a tenth and final plague on Egypt in terrible judgment—the death of the firstborn of every family. In order to spare the people of Israel, the Lord gave them specific directions to follow. God commanded them to take a lamb, keep it for four days, observe it, and make sure it was healthy. Then on that fourth day, in the evening, they were instructed to slaughter the lamb for the meal. They were to brush some of the blood from the Lamb on the top and sides of the doors of their homes. Then, gathered behind that symbol of the lamb's blood, the Lord told His people to eat this lamb as their evening meal. God said that this event would be a memorial for coming generations of the Lord's Passover, saying, "I will pass through the land of Egypt this night, and I will strike all the firstborn in the land of Egypt, both man and beast; and on all the gods of Egypt I will execute judgment: I am the Lord" (Exodus 12:12). God promised that He would "pass over" the homes wherever He saw the blood.

Have you ever wondered why there were any markings required at all? God certainly knows His people. He knew every house of every Hebrew slave throughout the land of Egypt. So, why did God do this? Why, then, this ritual? The Lord wanted His people then, and all people everywhere now, to understand through this event how sinful people (like you and me) are forgiven by a Holy and perfect God. That is the message of Passover—the forgiveness that comes through the blood of a sacrificial lamb.

I want to point out something in Exodus 12:3-5 that perhaps you have not noticed before.

> 3 Tell all the congregation of Israel that on the tenth day of this month every man shall take *a* lamb according to their fathers' houses, *a* lamb for a household. 4 And if the household is too small for a lamb, then he and his nearest neighbor shall take according to the number of persons; according to what each can eat you shall make your count for **the** lamb. 5 **Your** lamb shall be without blemish, a male a year old. You may take it from the sheep or from the goats,

Verse three says, "...every man shall take **a** lamb." Verse four says, "...you shall make your count for **the** lamb." And then verse five reads, "**Your** lamb shall be without blemish..."

*A lamb. **The** lamb. **Your** lamb.*

Why does God say it that way? Because He is reminding us that it is through *a* lamb that salvation will come. He is reminding us that it is not just any lamb; it is *the* Lamb. What did John the Baptist say when he saw Jesus coming to be baptized? "Behold, the Lamb of God, who takes away the sin of the world!" (John 1:29)

Jesus is *the* Lamb of God, but He must be *your* Lamb, your personal Savior. Jesus is the lamb provided for your salvation, and when you trust Him by faith, God's promise is still the same, "When I see the blood, I will pass over you." Through that first Passover, God demonstrated the way of eternal and personal salvation by sacrificing *a lamb*, which represented *the Lamb*, the Lamb of God, the Son, the Lord Jesus Christ, who can be *your Lamb*, for your salvation. Jesus can be your personal Lamb.

As a very young woman attending Cave Springs Baptist Church, just outside of Albany, Kentucky, my mom came to know Jesus as her personal lamb—the Lamb of God. By God's grace, she trusted in Jesus and was baptized in a profession of faith. My mother knew the Passover.

Not everyone remembers the time that they came to faith. I am glad that I can remember my own Passover. One Sunday night, in deep conviction for my sins, I sat on my bed and read a little booklet. I don't even know where this booklet came from, but it was entitled "God's Plan of Salvation." I read that booklet carefully and, taking a Bible out of my desk, I followed along with what the writer shared regarding the message of God's saving grace. Through reading the Scripture passages, the Lord revealed to my heart that I needed Christ and Christ alone.

I knelt by my bedside and called upon the Lord in prayer, and He blessed me with the assurance that, yes, indeed, Jesus was my Savior, my Lamb. In the middle of the night, I woke up my mom and dad and told them what had happened. We had a joyous praise celebration in that little bedroom of our old home in New Castle. I remember looking through my father's Bible shortly after his death and finding the faded copy of that little gospel booklet. He had saved it over all those years.

Now, how about *your* Passover? Have you experienced your own Passover? My friend, I want you to know something; it's the blood that makes you safe.

IT'S THE BLOOD
THAT MAKES YOU SAFE.

God said, "And when I see the blood, I will pass over you..." (Exodus 12:13). Centuries later, the apostle Paul declared with confidence, "There is therefore now no condemnation for those who are in Christ Jesus" (Romans 8:1). All people who are looking to Christ, trusting in His atoning sacrificial death as their only hope of salvation, are completely free from condemnation, forever. God, in His grace, grants that faith, that hope, that assurance, and through Christ we are made right with God, and the judgment on our sin has passed. Praise God, just as my mother wrote in her Bible, "It's the blood that makes you safe."

Then my mom wrote something else, "It's the Book that makes you sure."

IT'S THE BOOK
THAT MAKES YOU SURE.

Not long ago, during personal devotion, I read from Mark, Chapter 9. Maybe you recall this passage that records the failed attempts by Jesus' disciples to cast the demonic spirit out of a little boy. They try repeatedly, but they cannot do it. Jesus arrives, having just returned from the top of the mountain and experiencing His transfiguration. Learning of their failures, He commands, "'Bring him to me.' And they brought the boy to him" (Mark 9:19-20). Then Jesus said to the father of the boy, "'All things are possible for one who believes.' Immediately the father of the child cried out and said, 'I believe; help my unbelief!'" (Mark 9:23-24) Then, the Lord Jesus cast out the demonic spirit and returned the boy to his father.

Can you identify with that father? I know I can. "Lord, I believe but help my unbelief." We all struggle with unbelief. We all struggle with doubt. But how does the Lord help our unbelief? Well, the answer is exactly what my mother wrote in her Bible. *"It's the Book that makes you sure."* It's the Book, the Word of God, that produces faith, a sure and personal faith. In Romans 10:17, Paul reveals the source of faith.

So faith comes from hearing, and hearing through the word of Christ.

Admittedly, there is a mystery here. We do not understand how this works, but we are told by the Lord Himself that He uses His Word to create faith in us. If we desire more faith, we won't find it in our *experiences* or the experiences of others. We find faith and grow in faith through the *source of faith*—the Word of God. The Word of God brings saving faith.

**The law of the Lord is perfect,
reviving the soul;**
*the testimony of the Lord is sure,
making wise the simple;*
(Psalm 19:7)

8

The Lord's Word will do so much more than only *condemn* you. God will use His Word to *convert* you and revive your soul.

Many people struggle with the assurance of their salvation. Some people struggle because they cannot remember a moment or an experience when they first came to have faith in Jesus Christ. However, we don't gain assurance because we can go back to a moment in time, so many years ago, and remember that *experience*. That's not the place of assurance. Assurance is not found in our *experience*; it is found in the Word of God. The apostle John speaks about the assurance that comes from the message of the gospel:

I write these things to you who believe in the name of the Son of God, that you may know that you have eternal life.
(1 John 5:13)

Notice to whom John is writing. He doesn't say, "I've written these things to you pagans who don't believe a thing." No, he says, "I've written these things to you, who do believe in the name of the Son of God, that you may know...." The word "know" here means to know in personal reality and experience in your own life that you have eternal life. Where do you find assurance? You won't find it in an *event*. You will never find assurance in

9

thinking back to a time when you came forward at a gospel invitation at the close of a service, or by repeating a prayer, or by recalling some dramatic, spiritual moment. That memory can fade. Your emotions can change, but the Word of the Lord endures forever. The Bible is the anchor for our souls. The anchor is the Book that makes sure our faith. It's the Book that makes you sure and provides you with a sure faith. And it's the Book also that gives you a sure focus.

Have you ever attended a 3D movie where you must put on those special plastic glasses? If so, did you ever pull those glasses down to see what the movie looked like without them? The film is entirely out of focus and makes no sense. Then, when you put those glasses back on, wow! Everything is back in focus, and the film takes on meaning and perspective.

I remember our family once spending a day in Chattanooga, Tennessee, that included a visit to the IMAX theater. We all put on the special glasses to watch a brief film which included some scenes of flying birds. It was hilarious to watch the entire audience ducking left and right to avoid the "attacking birds!" What appeared to be reality was not reality at all. Ultimately, the only lens that brings life into true focus for us is the lens of God's Word. The Bible alone gives us a worldview that is accurate.

> *The law of the Lord is perfect,*
> *reviving the soul;*
> **the testimony of the Lord is sure,**
> **making wise the simple;**
> (Psalm 19:7)

Through God's Word, the simple becomes wise. There are little children, not yet three years old, that are wiser than some people with several Ph.D. degrees because here is what those little ones understand, "Jesus loves me this I know, for the Bible tells me so." Yes, indeed, "the testimony of the Lord is sure, making wise the simple." This is wisdom:

> *the precepts of the Lord are right,*
> *rejoicing the heart;*
> **the commandment of the Lord is**
> **pure,**
> **enlightening the eyes;**
> (Psalm 19:8)

As long as I can remember, my mother wore glasses. I inherited my eyesight from her. I have needed glasses since I was 19 years old. But I wear vanity glasses—contact lenses. My mom wore glasses but had 20/20 vision when discerning the truth. My older brother Lonnie and I still laugh when we think about Mom arguing with a TV news program as a commentator would share views with which she disagreed. Mom would start talking back to the television. She would loudly say, "That's just wrong." And then we would tease her, "Mom, you're talking to the television." And she would say, "I don't care; that's still wrong."

Mom had a unique saying she would share from time to time, "Listen, when this old world is rocking, the truth is going to stand." She was sure; she was confident. Mom possessed a sure focus. She wasn't questioning things that had already been settled in the Word of God. The principles that guided her life were not determined by public opinion or a changing society. "While this old world's rocking," (and it's rocking, right?) "...this truth is going to stand."

Heaven and earth will pass away, but my words will not pass away.
(Matthew 24:35)

IT'S THE BOOK
THAT MAKES YOU SURE.

The Book produces a sure faith. It provides a sure focus. And there is something else this book will do—it will place a sure foundation in your life.

About a year or two before I accepted a ministerial position in Knoxville, I served on the staff of a church in Findlay, Ohio. Just down the street from our church, another congregation built a lovely new auditorium. It was truly beautiful. However, about six months after that auditorium was built, cracks began to appear in the walls. Those cracks grew, and that church experienced an incredible problem because the company responsible for constructing the foundation had done shoddy work. The church was not built on a solid foundation.

So, you can understand why I watched closely as the workers formed the foundation of our new church building in Knoxville. I wanted to see for myself what would secure the large beams for our sanctuary. I was young and impatient then, and the building wasn't coming along fast enough for me. I'd go outside, day after day, and watch these rough, tough guys build the foundation and inspect what they were doing (as if I knew what was going on). It seemed to me that nothing was happening very quickly, and I was growing quite frustrated. Finally, one day I went to the job site and spoke to the superintendent, "You know, it seems as if this is taking so long." He looked at me with a look that only someone with all those years of building experience could give to a person who was clueless as to what needed to be done and said, "Preacher, it's like this. *You can't go high if you don't go deep.*" And in an instant, I understood. I replied, "Thank you very much. I think I will go back to my office now."

"*You can't go high if you don't go deep.*" I'm glad they went very deep, and I'm certain all those who attend our church are glad as well. The construction workers' carefulness in ensuring they went deep gave our congregation a sure foundation. We need to do the same with our lives.

How do you build a life that lasts? Physically, it is done by applying healthy habits like a good diet and plenty of exercise. But how do you build a life that lasts *spiritually*? Listen to the Master Builder.

> *Everyone then who hears these words of mine and does them will be like a wise man who built his house on the rock. And the rain fell, and the floods came, and the winds blew and beat on that house, but it did not fall, because it had been founded on the rock.*
> (Matthew 7:24-25)

His house was founded on the rock. The children sing the song "The wise man built his house upon the rock." It may be a child's song, but it shares grown-up wisdom. It is a foolish man who builds his house on the sand. Building on the Rock is how you build a life that really lasts. In fact, that is how you build a life that *outlasts you*—a life like my mom's.

Maybe your mother, or others who have influenced your life, have gone on, but even though they are dead, they still speak and influence you. Their lives last. When we live our lives based on the Bible, we live a life that leaves a legacy. My mother left a legacy, and not of money. I can assure you of that because I was the executor of her will. But she did leave a priceless legacy, one of faith, a life built on the foundation of the Bible.

A few days after her passing, I read my mother's Bible at her funeral at West Park Baptist Church, where I pastor. I recall reading and claiming some things in my mother's Bible that spoke to me. I claimed them for her children, their children, their children's children, and hopefully for all the generations to come.

"And as for me, this is my covenant with them," says the Lord: "My Spirit that is upon you, and my words that I have put in your mouth, shall not depart out of your mouth, or out of the mouth of your offspring, or out of the mouth of your children's offspring," says the Lord, "from this time forth and forevermore."
(Isaiah 59:21)

The prayer of my heart is that my children, my children's children, and their children's children, by God's grace, will speak the Words of the Lord forever.

As I thought about my mom and her legacy, I came across this passage that I claimed for myself. I sometimes refer to this as the "psalm of the senior saint," and I hate to say it, but I think I am one now. These words are so much more powerful to me today, nearly 18 years after my mother's passing. Here is what King David prayed in Psalm 71:17-18:

> *O God, from my youth you have taught me,*
> *and I still proclaim your wondrous deeds.*
> *So even to old age and gray hairs,*
> *O God, do not forsake me,*
> *until I proclaim your might to another*
> *generation,*
> *your power to all those to come.*

That legacy should be the heartbeat of every senior believer in Jesus Christ. "Now that we're old, don't abandon me. Let me proclaim your power. Let not my words be bitter words, complaining words, words of doubt, but in my gray hair, let me proclaim your mighty miracles for all who will come after me to a new generation."

Mom wrote, "It's the blood that makes you safe. It's the book that makes you sure," and then finally, she wrote, "It's obedience that makes you happy."

IT'S OBEDIENCE
THAT MAKES YOU HAPPY.

I thought, "Poor Mom. She didn't get it. I mean, it's as straightforward as it can be. Just reach for one of those magazines at the checkout counter. It's broadcast on talk radio all the time. How could you miss this on television? It's plastered all over social media. How could you have missed it, Mom? It is the *beautiful* who are happy! It is the *wealthy* who are happy! It is the *successful* who are happy!"

Poor Mom. She just didn't get it. No. She got it. And here is what she got:

> *...the rules of the Lord are true,*
> *and righteous altogether.*
> *More to be desired are they than gold,*
> *even much fine gold;*
> *sweeter also than honey*
> *and drippings of the honeycomb.*
> *Moreover, by them is your servant warned;*
> *in keeping them there is great reward.*
> (Psalm 19:9-11)

My friend, virtue is its own reward. Obedience to God is its own reward. Jesus so wanted us to understand this because it is completely contrary to what the world teaches. He so wanted us to get it that He not only told us, He showed us. Do you remember John 13?

Jesus rose from the table at the last supper, the last Passover, took a basin, and filled it with water. He wrapped a towel around his waist, then washed His disciples' dirty feet. That ritual cleansing of the feet should have happened *before* the meal. Why did it not happen *before* the meal? Because none of the disciples were willing to take the place of a servant. So, Jesus did the servant's task. John, who was seated next to Jesus, decades later recorded what Jesus said:

If you know these things,
blessed are you if you do them.
(John 13:17)

What are "these things?" "These things" are serving others, putting others before ourselves, being concerned about our brothers and sisters, and being available for people who are hurting. Jesus wants us to do what we can to help others. We may get a little messy, the water into which we place our hands may be a little dirty and murky, and it may splatter on us, but we can be assured of something. If we do this, we will be blessed. We will be happy.

My mother knew much heartache in her long life of 81 years. As I think back, she was a woman of sorrows and acquainted with grief. When she was just a young teenage girl, she became the caregiver for all her younger brothers and sisters because her mother had experienced a complete physical and nervous collapse and was incapacitated for the rest of her life. From when my mother was just a young teenager, she was, for all intents and purposes, the mother in the house.

She married my dad at 24, and when she was 25 years old, she gave birth to a severely disabled son, my brother, Lloyd. She cared for all his daily needs. You can imagine what that was like. For the next 49 years, until my father passed, my mother lovingly cared for my brother. When my father died, Mom could no longer care for my brother alone. Then, she knew the grief of seeing her 49-year-old son leave home to be cared for by others, recognizing that she would probably never see him again. In addition to this, my mother lost a little boy at birth, my brother Stephen. She lived a life that knew chronic pain and illness. She buried a son. She buried her husband. She buried eight brothers and sisters. Yet, my mom smiled a lot, had a wonderful frequent laugh, and our home was filled with joy. It was not a place of gloom and doom.

My mother experienced the joy we can all experience as believers in Jesus because it's not *circumstances* that make us happy—it's *obedience*. God chose a hard and difficult path for Mom, and she struggled along that path patiently. But she was *obedient*, and she was happy in the Lord.

I sat by her bed for the last two days of her life. My mom was very alert, but it seemed as if she was far away. She was continually looking off, and she had the most beautiful and serene smile on her face.

Before my mother passed, I told my wife, Susan, "You know, Mom's at peace." And from some of the things she said and by her countenance, I truly believe she knew her journey was complete. Heaven was already in her heart. How could that be when she had been so ill and life had been so hard for so long? Well, let me tell you:

IT'S THE BLOOD THAT MAKES YOU SAFE.
IT'S THE BOOK THAT MAKES YOU SURE.
IT'S OBEDIENCE THAT MAKES YOU HAPPY.

Amen, Mom. Amen.

These are timeless words written in *My Mother's Bible,* and I pray they will be inscribed on your heart today.

Lord, I pray for all the moms reading these words that you minister to them with grace. God, I pray that their legacy be incredible. I pray for their children and their children's children. I pray, Lord, until you come, even if it's a thousand generations, let the legacies of these women of faith go on and on. I pray not just for mothers but for all those who choose a faithful legacy that lasts. Lord, we are so bombarded, so prone to wander, so susceptible to the lies of the enemy and our own flesh regarding what constitutes a life that matters. Lord, may we see that it is in Christ alone that we have an abundant life. Only in Jesus can we have a life that lasts through these days and into the days of eternity. Lord, I ask that everyone who reads these words seek their own Passover with all their heart as they look to the blood of the Lamb, Jesus Christ, for everything. Oh, Lord, thank you that the promise is still there, the promise that when we look to the blood, you look to the blood, and you pass over judgment. We praise you for that. And Lord, help us daily to say, "Take anything else but give us Jesus."

ABOUT CLIMBING ANGEL
PUBLISHING

Climbing Angel Publishing exists for the purpose of sharing stories of hope and encouragement, aiding in the gathering together of community, and supporting the process of betterment. The following books are available at ClimbingAngel.com and major bookstores.

ADULT BOOKS: (Romans 8:28-30)

In His Image by Sam Polson
(English, Romanian, & Mandarin)
By Faith by Sam Polson (English & Romanian)
My Birthday Gift to Jesus by Lisa Soland
Without Ceasing by Dr. Dennis Davidson
SonLight: Daily Light from the Pages of God's Word
by Sam Polson
Corona Victus: Conquering the Virus of Fear
by Sam Polson (English & Romanian)
Art Bushing: His Diary, Letters, & Photographs of WWII
by Art Bushing
Art & Dotty: His Diary, Their Letters & Photographs of
WWII by Art Bushing
Trimisul by Stan Johnson (Romanian)
Life Changing Prayer by Sam Polson
The Climbing Angel Christmas Treasury, variety of authors
J. Calvin Coolidge: Letters from the Korean War
by J. Calvin Coolidge

Stories from Kingman, AZ: The Heart of Historic Route 66
by Loren B. Wilson
*Pathways: Ancient Paths from the Pages of the Old
Testament* by Sam Polson
Jesus is Alive! by Mike Sager
My Mother's Bible by Sam Polson

CHILDREN'S BOOKS: (Philippians 4:8)

The Christmas Tree Angel by Lisa Soland
The Unmade Moose by Lisa Soland
Thump by Lisa Soland
Somebunny To Love by Lisa Soland
(English & Mandarin)
The Truth About God's Rainbow by Lisa Soland
God's Promises by Lisa Soland
The Boy & The Bagel Necklace by Lisa Soland
God's Hands and Feet by Lisa Soland
I Like To Be Quiet by Joni Caldwell
Wheels Off! by Karlie Saumier
Ella's Trip of a Lifetime by Melanie Ewbank
Because You Are Mine by Gayle Childress Greene
Jeremy Plays the Blues by Amy Oden Simpson
Bad Hair Day by Jasmyne Simpkins
I Like To Read by Joni Caldwell
Trunks Up! by Karlie Saumier
Perusha's Paradise by Bette Reed Smith
Ruby and the Treasure Within by Tonya Celeste Hobbs
Abby, the Wonder Dog & her Warrior Princess
by Melanie Ewbank
The Christmas Coat by Lisa Soland

www.ingramcontent.com/pod-product-compliance
Lightning Source LLC
Chambersburg PA
CBHW051604120626
46551CB00013B/1666